MEMOIRS

OF

CHARLES CAMPBELL,

AT PRESENT PRISONER IN THE JAIL OF GLASGOW.

INCLUDING

HIS ADVENTURES AS A SEAMAN, AND AS AN OVERSEER IN THE WEST INDIES.

WRITTEN BY HIMSELF.

TO WHICH IS APPENDED

AN ACCOUNT OF HIS TRIAL

BEFORE THE

CIRCUIT COURT OF JUSTICIARY,

At Glasgow, 27th April, 1826.

Price One Shilling.

GLASGOW:

JAMES DUNCAN & Co. 8, WILSON STREET,
J. T. SMITH & Co., HUNTER'S SQUARE, EDINBURGH,
AND JAMES DUNCAN, LONDON.

MDCCCXXVIII.

MEMOIRS

OF

CHARLES CAMPBELL,

AT PRESENT PRISONER IN THE JAIL OF GLASGOW.

INCLUDING

HIS ADVENTURES AS A SEAMAN, AND AS AN OVERSEER
IN THE WEST INDIES.

WRITTEN BY HIMSELF.

TO WHICH IS APPENDED,

AN ACCOUNT OF HIS TRIAL

BEFORE THE

CIRCUIT COURT OF JUSTICIARY,

At GLASGOW, 27th APRIL, 1826.

GLASGOW:

JAMES DUNCAN & Co. 8, WILSON STREET,
J. T. SMITH & Co., HUNTER'S SQUARE, EDINBURGH,
AND JAMES DUNCAN, LONDON.

MDCCCXXVIII.

PREFACE.

It is with feelings of extreme reluctance that I submit the following narrative to the eye of the public. The situation in which I am placed—one of peculiar privation —could alone prevail on me to overcome my scruples. To a mind of ordinary delicacy, it is always painful to speak of one's self; but I trust the candid and generous reader will pardon my presumption, if, in my lonely and destitute condition, I have been induced to listen to the suggestion of friends, and drawn out an outline of my life, in the hope that the proceeds of its publication might tend to mitigate the sufferings of my long-protracted imprisonment. This, I freely acknowledge, is my object in the present work. I have not written these sheets under any feeling that my life was worth recording; yet the dreadful circumstance that marked one part of it, and that must affect all which is to come, may render it interesting to some, and awake the sympathy of the truly just and good.

I am naturally led to expect that some countenance will be bestowed me, at least from one quarter. My late occupation as a Cotton-Spinner in this neighbourhood induces me to look to that class of workers with a kind of fraternal confidence; and, while I acknowledge my obligations to them for past favours, I wish to remind them that I was one of their number in the day of their political conflict, and, that my efforts were directed in defence of their disputed rights, during the most arduous of their struggles. I still wish to congratulate them on the peaceable and manly deportment with which they bore their sufferings, during a period of five months, in which not a single instance of violence occurred; and I trust that on all future occasions of the kind, they will regulate themselves by the same laudable and constitutional spirit, and so put it out of the power of Calumny itself to brand them with the epithets which the public prints were once liberal in bestowing.

I have only to add, that, in writing the subjoined narrative, my main object was to adhere to truth; and being no hero myself, I thought it better to speak of what I saw, and felt, and thought in the world, rather than make a parade of all I did and suffered.

Had I been inclined, I might have swelled the present pamphlet to an ordinary sized volume; but it would have been presuming too much on the good-nature of my readers. Even as it is, I beg they will not look grudgingly upon it; but consider that, while it may afford them a few minutes' relaxation, they are relieving the privations of a fellow-creature, who, after two years of weary imprisonment, has no higher wish than to enjoy more freely the fresh air and blessed light of heaven.

GLASGOW JAIL,
Feb. 22d, 1828.

*** The account of the Trial is taken verbatim from the Glasgow Free Press Newspaper of the 29th April, 1826.

MEMOIRS.

I was born on the 2d April, 1793, in a small village of Argyllshire; its name is Tarbert; it is situated on the isthmus of Kintyre, in the parish of Killcalmonel. My ancestors were of the family of Craignish. During the invasion of Montrose into the county of Argyll, the first of my paternal ancestors who settled in Kintyre, was, previous to that event, made a prisoner by the soldiers of that heroic General, and confined with others of his clan, (whose conduct or opposition had rendered them obnoxious to the invaders,) in a large barn, for the time being, there to await the decision of their enraged captors. My ancestor, whose name was Charles, overhearing the sentinels at the door discoursing together, imbibed the intelligence that all the prisoners would be put to death next morning. He was naturally alarmed, but mustering all the courage that desperation could supply, he took his knife, and in the dead of night, cut the hinge off by which the hurdle door was suspended. He then made a sudden leap at his enemies, the sentinels, knocked down two of them, and sought refuge in flight. But an alarm was soon raised, and he became the object of immediate pursuit. Finding himself hard pressed and despairing of making his escape good by flight, he concealed himself among some brushwood till his pursuers came up, and then availing himself of the darkness of the night, mingled with the party, and for a short while, succeeded in imposing a belief that he was one of their own number by joining the hue and cry, and shouting as vehemently as any of them, " Catch the black Campbell!" the agnomen by which he was usually distinguished. In a short time, however, the moon breaking through a cloud laid him open to suspicion just when they had reached the brink of a small lake of which he well knew the geography. There to avoid being massacred on the spot, he plunged from the steep bank into the watery element, and concealed himself among the reeds and long grass that fringed its margin. His pursuers now concluding that the water had effected all, if not more than they themselves intended, thought it superfluous to attempt any thing further, and therefore left him to his fate. He escaped unhurt, and his daring attempt was the means of affording liberty to his fellow prisoners, who, finding the door of the barn open, and the enemy gone, decamped without obstruction. Shortly af-

A

terwards, the said Charles settled in the farm of Escart, within two miles of Tarbert. Part of the dwelling-house is still extant, and distinguished by a range of Druidical pillars, the most remarkable of the kind in that district. Here my forefathers lived in direct succession, without any local change of abode, down to the days of my grandfather, who died a young man, leaving however, a pretty numerous family, all of whom are now extinct: most of their descendants have emigrated to America, where many of them live in comparative affluence.

When I was but an infant, my father quitting the Highlands, settled in Johnstone, a handsome and populous village of Renfrewshire, where he was employed during the remainder of his life, in the warehouse of a Cotton-mill. He was a man remarkable for nothing but his unaffected piety, and the unconquerable integrity of his heart. By him I was early and earnestly instructed in the principles and practice of religion, and continually admonished of the danger of tampering with vice, even when she assumed the exterior of virtue. His favourite maxim was to preserve an unshaken integrity through all the transactions of life; and, to speak truth, he was the only man I ever knew that was as honest as he professed to be. Though he lived in this, his heart was in another world. No advantage, no argument would palliate, in his eyes, a dishonest act, however trifling. He saw no wealth, no treasure in this world, but the possession of an upright heart, and used to say, that a man that feared God could never be poor. His whole soul was continually, especially in the latter part of his life, occupied with the glad tidings of Salvation contained in the Gospel. His religion was purely abstract; about differences of sects and controversies, he cared nothing; he knew as little of them as a child; and only wondered that pious men should occupy themselves with such frivolities.

By this excellent parent I was early sent to school, and between his private tuition and that of my first schoolmaster, I could read English fluently, and even write at six or seven years of age. To instruct me in the Gælic language, of which he was a perfect master, after giving me some lessons, he resolved on sending me home to my native shire, when I was put to school at the village of Lagavullin, under the auspices of Mr. Beaton, still, so far as I know, master of the same school.

After remaining here sometime under the hospitable roof of a paternal relative, I was again recalled to the Low Country. My father shortly after my return, began to fail in body, and to sink under the pressure of a laborious asthma, which so much enfeebled his constitution that he was no longer able to follow his avocation. I was now sent to a Cotton-mill where I could earn about eight or ten shillings a-week. After this period, all the means of inruction I ever possessed resulted from my own exertions. I early imbibed taste for reading, and the first trifling sum that lay in my hands, as a redun-ncy over the immediate exigencies of the family, was laid out as subscription oney at a circulating library in a neighbouring town. After the toils of the y were past, the little I could snatch from sleep was devoted to the perusal such books as the library could supply. Often have I trudged, in the dark nter nights, a distance of several miles, through wind and rain, to get my oks exchanged. I read much of History, Biography, Voyages, Travels, most all the old Dramatic Poets, of whom I was passionately fond, and the jority of the English Classics. In this manner I laid in a considerable ck of miscellaneous knowledge while yet very young, and the contempla-n of the time thus spent has ever been a source of unfeigned satisfaction. I now became a member of a society whose real object was to debate on rary subjects. It consisted of twelve members; we met once a-week, and winding up the debate, a question was voted for the subject of the ensuing eting. Matters of a religious and political nature were absolutely excluded. e presidentship went by rotation; and our meetings, after the question was posed of, broke up with some amusing story, or song from the chair. The iety consisted chiefly of artisans and mechanics, such as had a taste for ading and literary pursuits; and some of its members have since attained to uations of profit and respectability both at home and abroad. One, in par-ular, is at present a Lecturer on Philosophy, and Editor of a respectable edical Journal. Our regulations were nearly similar to those of the Mauch-n club, on which the name of Burns has conferred immortality. The mem-rs, however, were not obliged, like those of the bachelor's club, to live in gle blessedness. Once a-year we celebrated the anniversary of our Institu-on, by holding a night of festal glee, to the mysteries of which every mem-r had it in his option to introduce a neutral person, whose sentiments were t suspected to be in hostility with our patron goddesses—Nature and Art. e spent these nights in the most tempered and social harmony, toasting the emories of all the renowned worthies of our native land. We read essays, ade speeches, and sung songs; the diversity was heightened by recitations om favourite authors, original pieces, sometimes of our own composition; and ow and then, an interlude of soft music, breathed from a couple or two of ell-toned flutes. The night was one of relaxation, not of debate; of rational, ough somewhat uproarious enjoyment. The ties of close friendship had nited every heart as a link in an indissoluble chain, which no tyrant but time uld break; every link was gold, and that will never rust even when ried—Peace to the manes of the past! There are groups and assemblages the memory of man, on which, like the flowery Oasis of the desert, it would be little profit to dwell, but on which, as we travel onward, we are often tempted to look back. The society continued in existence for many years. Being the only thing of the kind that was ever instituted in the village, it experienced a good deal of opposition at its first outset; but confident of the rectitude and utility of the principle on which it was founded, the members continued their meetings through good and evil report, and finally triumphed, establishing the credit of the club. The dispersion of its members to different quarters of the world was, I believe, the final cause of its dissolution. It was a cheap school of pleasure and profit, well supplied with books, and conducted almost without any expense. As we never met in a public-house above once or twice a-year, it led to no habits of irregularity or dissipation. On the contrary, the moral truths and maxims that naturally sprung from the frequent exercise of intellect to which it gave rise, formed of themselves a kind of bulwark that excluded meaner pursuits, and kept the mind from deteriorating, by keeping its eye so constantly fixed on the grand, though confusedly moving panorama of great and interesting objects. To men toiling in the humblest walks of life, the approaches to knowledge were no doubt circuitous, and in many instances, the want of time, books, and legitimate guides, left them like way-fairers storm-steaded; still however, they had the mountain of knowledge in view, and the distance seemed only to heighten the sublimity. A taste for knowledge and science is of such noble origin, as to confer a kind of lustre on its humblest possessor. There is something in the pleasure it yields so superior to the gratification arising from common place topics, and the tittle tattle of life, as to rank the poorest gleaner in the harvest of literature, at least a degree above the herd of bipeds, whose whole range of intellect is circumscribed to the science of profit and loss, and the mere mechanical operations of life and nature. The highest security of enjoyment that the latter can attain to is vested in the power of fortune, and may perish in an hour; but the treasures of knowledge are of an unfading nature, and their value becomes rather enhanced than diminished, by adversity. Thus the votary of intellectual delight can never be rendered absolutely desolate by the operations of chance; for even when fortune and friends forsake him, he has still something left in the treasures of his mind, to console him either in sorrow or solitude. It must be to a mind of this kind the poet alludes when he says—

> Sweet are the uses of adversity,
> Which, like the toad, ugly and venomous,
> Wears yet a precious jewel in its head.

The lover of learning, however straitened his circumstances, or rugged his condition, has yet a source of enjoyment within himself that the world never dreams of; and, perhaps, when common observers think him unhappy, his mind is contemplating objects of which they can have but a faint conception. Perhaps he is solving a problem of Euclid, or soaring with Newton amidst the planetary world, and endeavouring to discover the nature and properties of that invisible attraction by which the Almighty mind has subjected inanimate matter to laws that resemble the operations of intelligence: or descending from the harmony of the spheres, he contemplates the principle of animal life, and explores the intricate labyrinths of physiological phenomena. If tired or disappointed in his physical researches, he has the mighty and sublime region of mind to revel in. Pursuing the footsteps of Locke and of Reid, he traces the origin of his own ideas, feelings, and passions: or tired with the labour of tracing effects to their first causes, and baffled in his attempts at analyzing the complex machinery of the human soul, he unbends the wing of his imagination, and solaces his weary mind in the delightful gardens of the classic muse. Poetry and music have a wild charm over the heart: like moonlight, they cast a pleasing disguise over the realities of nature, and soften, by their mellow tints and colourings, those asperities of misluck and cankered occurrences, that usually irritate a feeling mind in their plain prose and matter of fact appearance. Thus, a person fond of reading has always either a useful or amusing companion at command. When tired of the pages of the Stagyrite, he can fly to the court of Meonidas.

> 'Tis he who gives my breast a thousand pains,
> Can make me feel each passion that he feigns;
> Enrage, compose, with more than magic art;
> With pity and with terror tear my heart,
> And snatch me o'er the earth, or through the air,
> To Thebes, to Athens, when he will, and where.

I have been induced to make these remarks on the pleasure incidental to a reading mind, as there are many persons not devoid of good sense, who affect to despise any pursuit that diverts the attention from the main business of life, without having money for its immediate object. These persons, in their own eyes, are certainly the only true philosophers; they would not, like the dog crossing the river, drop the bone from their mouth, to grasp at the shadow. Money in their estimation is the true philosopher's stone. Such persons are disposed to be critical on the waste of time occasioned by literary pursuits, which they reckon idle application in those who are obliged to earn their bread by the sweat of their brow, without once reflecting, that they themselves frequently squander their precious hours in pursuits and amusements not only less profitable, but altogether trite and frivolous. The members of our little club felt this truth too forcibly to abandon the path our institution had chalked out. We were every whit as well disposed, and ready to pursue the duties of our various avocations as others were, and we enjoyed a rational relaxation from the drudgery of life, to which our detractors were perfect strangers. These honest people branded us with the designation of atheists, poets, and play-actors; and their officious gossiping was to me the source of many a domestic lecture. No poor devil was ever more tortured, or persecuted, for his attachment to books than I was. Every cross accident —every misfortune, that chequered my early life, was ascribed to my love of books, and the influence of our club. My father, however, never forbade me to attend it: he felt pleasure in observing that my religious principles were unshaken, and uncontaminated; and he was far from being displeased with the books he found in circulation among us. His death, however, which happened when the society was in its infancy, left me to follow the bent of my own mind within our domestic circle. I was then freed from the terror of a severe censor; but I had also lost my best counsellor and friend.

Previous to his death, he bound me apprentice to a trade for which I had no great liking. My master finding his business not very prosperous, thought, I believe, that it would be a good job to get the penalty stipulated in my indenture, in case of failure on my part to perform the articles of agreement. He, therefore, took occasion to use me rather harshly, and one time, when I resented his conduct by a spirited expression, he struck me, and turned me out of doors. I now considered myself at liberty, and resisted every persuasion of my friends to return to my work. When I found them urgent, I listened to the suggestions of my own heart rather than to their arguments, and happening to meet with an intimate friend, who was then about to leave the village on a romantic excursion, which he had concocted in his own fertile brain, he invited me to accompany him—a proposal to which I not only agreed, but embraced with enthusiasm. I immediately eloped without the knowledge of any other person; and after making a very agreeable, and not uninteresting tour, through one of the most romantic districts in Scotland, returned home again at the end of six or seven weeks. My master got me immediately apprehended, and to save myself from jail, I was obliged to sign a bill for a penalty of ten pounds. Although our family was but poor, and my mother a widow, this fellow exacted the full penalty, with the most merciless and uncompromising avidity. In order to facilitate the object of payment, and to get rid of the fellow's importunity, my former landlord and cautioner advised me to endeavour to dispose of a small manuscript of poetry by subscription. The advice was taken, and the manuscript sent immediately to the press. This project also failed, and involved my cautioner and myself in new difficulties. The volume was printed, but from bad management it never came to be disposed of. From this period, in spite of every endeavour after well-doing, my life has been one continued series of disappointments.

I now turned my thoughts on going to sea—the usual resort of the unfortunate. Accordingly, through the interest of a friend, I engaged with a captain bound for the West Indies in 1812, and on the 16th of February set sail from the Tail of the Bank. We experienced, on our entrance into the Atlantic Ocean, a most tremendous storm. The sea was literally transformed into aqueous mountains, whose curled tops hung over us with a stupendous aspect of sublimity. On the other hand, every yawning gulph, deep as Cocytus, threatened instant and eternal annihilation. It was beautiful, but terrible, to contemplate the gigantic billows hanging over us, roaring and waving their trembling crests, feathered with pompous spray, and stained with all the vivid tints of the rainbow. The ship was tossed from side to side most rudely, but she floated with all the buoyancy of a cork. One night (for the storm lasted many days) when the spirit of the tempest shrieked through our tackle and cordage, and when all around us was dark as the passage of Æneas to hell, a tremendous sea struck the ship, and for some moments completely overwhelmed her. The long boat was torn up from the ring bolts that fastened it to the deck, the jolly boat was swept from the mizzen chains, the bulwarks were completely demolished from the stern to the waste, and the huge spars on deck thrown loose from their lashings. I was at the time in my hammock in the forecastle: the rush of the water down the hatch was like the noise of thunder, and for a moment the dubious light of the firmament was extinguished in the passage. A Dutchman lay in the hammock along side of mine. He leaped out, and exclaimed—" By Cot Almighty the ship is foundered! I'll be damned for it is! We are all lost every soul of us!" After a fearful pause, a seaman came to the fore hatch, and knocking with a handspike, shouted—" All hands—the ship's a wreck!" We sprung on deck; the carpenter sounded the pump, and sung out—" Seven feet water." At this dreadful news the crew and passengers were thunderstruck, and one of these, a member of the worthy firm of the ship's owners, began to wring his hands and tear his hair, crying—" Oh my good ship :" but his eagerness to get out the boat, showed that it was not the ship, but his conscience that troubled him. The boat, however, was damaged; but, at any rate, she would not have lived a moment in the rage of that sea. The captain at length expressed his doubts of the accuracy of the carpenter's experiment in sounding, and going back to the cabin, had the line rubbed over with chalk. During this fearful suspense, between life and death, all was silence; the boldest on board seemed to hold his breath in the act of listening to the result. The captain sounded, and the joyful tidings were announced of only three or four inches water in the pump. All now felt relieved: the distressed owner drowned his lamentations in a bumper, and the sailors began their old swearing again. Eleven of our water casks were stove by the rolling of the ship. A council of war was held on the expediency of returning to some port for a fresh supply of water; but it was finally resolved that we should proceed on our voyage. We were eleven weeks in crossing the Atlantic. At length we arrived safe in the Island of New Providence, lying at no great distance from the first land (another of the Bahama Islands) that cheered the drooping hopes of Columbus in his search for a new world. I was disappointed in my views of a situation at New Providence, and, therefore, returned to Scotland in the same ship.

The next year, 1813, I sailed for the Island of Jamaica. I had a letter of recommendation from the brother of one of the owners of the vessel who lived in the Island, and therefore felt confident that this knight errant voyage would prove more fortunate than the last. On our way we put into Cork, in expectation of a convoy; but after remaining there a fortnight or three weeks, we were necessitated to proceed on our voyage alone. We had eight passengers on board, who kept fiddling and dancing the whole voyage. When off the coast of Portugal we had a pretty severe gale, which for some time interrupted their gaiety; but the most serious occurrence was a heavy sea, that swept away our cambouse and cook-house, without the least ceremony. The cook, a black fellow, was within at the time preparing breakfast, but he had the presence of mind to step out, and take hold of the main chains, just as the moveable building took its final departure. We soon made the Island of Barmuda in the West Indies;

> And passing through the isles that lie
> Like cloudlets in a summer's sky,

we were attacked by an American Privateer off Navassa rock, at the west end of St. Domingo. This put fiddling out of the heads of our Glasgow dandies a second time; but the skilful management of our captain, and the darkness of the night, finally freed them from putting their trembling courage to the test of action. We arrived all safe at Montego Bay, a handsome sea-port town of Jamaica. Here I forwarded my letter of recommendation, but it had no effect. Having discharged our European cargo, we loaded with wood and other articles, with which we proceeded to Kingston. In this trip we had a number of West Indian dandies on board, who were in great spirits for a sea fight, boasting how they would treat the first Yanky Privateer that should come in their way. Immediately a coasting sloop hove in sight. It was a fine moonlight night, a calm sea, and almost no wind. Our vessel was an armed schooner of eight guns. The captain and mate, being both under the influence of Bacchus at the time, were willing to give the dandies a specimen of their admiralship, and after clearing the deck for an engagement, ordered the guns to be loaded. The dandies now began to blanch; some of them slunk back to the cabin, others, who were ashamed to be thought cowards, kept the deck, but with looks that clearly indicated their agitation. The sloop advanced—it was midnight—the captain ran to and fro calling on the absent dandies, damning them to stand to their guns. He then hailed the sloop, but no answer. The next word was fire, and we poured a few shots into her. The sloop bore away—muskets, pistols, and cutlasses, were then put in requisition. We pursued—the sloop immediately hove to, when the master informed us that he was no Yanky, but a poor Creole drugger, and then calmly requested our address. Our captain replied, that his vessel was the None-Such, and with Quixotic complacency proceeded on his voyage. The master of the drugger afterwards prosecuted for damages, and, I believe, obtained something.

Having disloaded at Kingston, we returned to Montego Bay. Here our crew were seized with the yellow fever, and were carried ashore, one after another, till only three remained, and I was one of these. Two of us felt the approach of the fearful malady one night while we were assailed by a hurricane, which in that climate is a dreadful commotion of the elements of heaven, and earth, and sea. Our vessel drifted from her anchoring ground, and snapping both her chain and hempen cable, was cast ashore among the Bogue Islands, at the mouth of the river Styx—not the Styx that Orpheus and Æneas crossed, although a greater than Orpheus or Æneas was once shipwrecked on its muddy shore—the immortal Columbus. By the assistance of a Negro and two Portuguese, I was landed and conveyed to the house of a Negro woman in Montego Bay, where I was put to bed, and treated with the greatest kindness, till I recovered of the fever under which I then laboured. I scarcely remember any thing of this circumstance, except, that on being put to bed, the house was unroofed by the violence of the tempest, and the rain poured down on me in torrents. I was immediately carried to another apartment. During my illness I was attended by a medical gentleman from Glasgow, who predicted to my nurse that the fever would prove fatal on the fourth or fifth night. The event proved the acuteness of his sagacity; for, as I afterwards learned from my nurse herself, she approached my bed-side on the predicted day, and found me cold and breathless. Concluding that the vital spark had fled, she proceeded to perform the last office to my apparently lifeless remains, when, putting her hand on my breast, she felt my heart still beating. She then took a phial of the tincture of Cayenne pepper, with which she embrocated my breast, and finally poured some of it into my ear : I immediately recovered the power of respiration. From that period the fever left me, and I gradually recovered. Thus, by the kind attention of this poor African, I found myself restored to life.

The doctor now calling, told me the danger was over, and to my enquiries for the captain and mate he answered, that they were doing well; but when he found me past the danger of a relapse, told me that they were both buried.

The treatment in yellow fever consists in keeping the bowels open, by administering frequent dozes of submuriate of mercury; and in promoting perspiration, by the plentiful use of brandy diluted with water.

After I was so far recovered as to bear sitting in a chair under the piazza, my attention was one day arrested by the figure of a person, meagre and wan, approaching towards me from the opposite side of the street. He had a handkerchief about his head, and a staff in his hand on which he leaned dejectedly. On coming nearer, his countenance assumed a ghastly smile. He advanced hurriedly to within a few paces of my seat on the piazza—stopped—leaned on his stick—and exclaimed—" My God! is this you?" It was Phillip Gray, the only survivor of all my shipmates. I rose and shook him by the hand.

The day previous to his falling sick he had quarrelled with the captain. The captain struck him for some trivial fault, my shipmate returned the blow, and a battle ensued, in which poor Phillip had the worst of it, on account of his opponent seizing a mallet, and knocking him down with it. Phillip, said I, have you heard of the captain's fate. Phillip looked me in the face—" Yes," replied he, " his soul is in hell ;" and, seizing a glass of rum which my kind hostess had set before us, he drank—" Damnation to all tyrants !"

We took a ramble through the town together, escorted by two or three Negroes. In the fulness of our joy we entered a spirit shop, and drank one gill of rum between us. The liquor had such an effect upon our exhausted bodies, that we returned staggering tipsy, and, I believe, it was one of the happiest days of our lives.

Being still weak with the effects of the fever, and finding our lodgings very expensive, we made application to the proper authorities, and were admitted as convalescents into the town's hospital. The hospital was pleasantly situated on the verge of the ocean, about a mile from the town of Montego Bay, and skirted everywhere on the land side with woods, mountains, and pastures. The discipline of the hospital did not confine us within doors during the day; we had therefore an opportunity of traversing the country in whatever direction we pleased, and to as great a distance as our strength, and the intervals between meals, would authorise us to venture. During our stay here we had many pleasant rambles among the woods, which everywhere abound with fruit. Here I was first struck with the marks of devastation the late hurricane had imprinted on the face of Nature; for we met not only huge trees torn up by the roots, but observed that those on the tops of the hills were stripped of their entire foliage, standing like the scathed pine in Milton's description, to which he compares the ruin of the arch fiend, stately but bare, without a single leaf. This afforded us sufficient proof of the terrible force of the aerial element in these dreadful commotions, when the heavens, as it were, loose their balance.

The sick list of our hospital consisted of only four persons, and we usually sallied out in a body. The exercise, fresh air, and change of objects, which the liberties of the institution afforded us, had a salutary influence on our health, for we gradually recovered our strength and spirits, and within the limits of a single month, we were all enabled to resume the active duties of life.

For want of better luck we now shipped on board of a drugger or coasting vessel, and cruized from one port to another, carrying chingles, staves, hoops, boards, and whatever came in our way. In this duty Phillip and I had little to do, but guide the vessel at sea. In harbour, the whole toil of loading and unloading fell on the Negroes. The master of the sloop was a Mulatto, a man of a gay and amorous disposition. He had a sable sweetheart in every port and cove, and whenever the sea breeze blew hard, he was sure to put into the first creek, that he might have an interview with one of his black dulcineas of the woods. In these adventures we sometimes accompanied him, and were generally kindly entertained. After remaining on shore most of the day, we used to weigh anchor in the evening; for the weather is then always moderate, and we had the advantage of the rock wind, or land breeze, which blows from the centre of the Island towards every point of the compass. After making several trips with this captain of the yellow countenance, we left him, in order to look after a situation more lucrative. Phillip took shipping for Kingston, and I proceeded to Martha Brae. Here I was perfectly a stranger, and had but little money; however, I met one of our old passengers from Greenock, who was a wealthy merchant, and had a splendid store in this town. He gave me a kind reception, and treated me to a glass of rum. He then advised me to stop in town a few days, and promised to procure me the situation of book-keeper on some neighbouring estate. I acquiesced, but after waiting and wearying till my little stock of money was expended, he still put me off. I went on board a ship in the harbour, and wrought for my victuals a few days, expecting that something would cast up.

Here, during my stay on board, a circumstance occurred, that set the humanity of West Indian captains and planters in a prominent point of view. A male Negro, a slave, about twenty years of age, came on board to dispose of some fruit. A quarrel ensued between the Negro and one of the sailors about the price of the article which was the subject of barter. The mate of the ship interfered, and on learning the cause of the dispute, was so enraged against the Negro, that he took up a piece of wood, and began to beat him most unmercifully. The poor sufferer wept, and called for quarter; but finding there was none to be had at the hands of this white barbarian, in despair he leaped overboard, and was immediately drowned. Had this happened in any Christian country, it certainly would have been made the subject of legal inquiry; nothing of this kind, however, took place. The captain of the ship paid the master of the Negro a sum of eighty pounds as an equivalent for the loss of his slave, and the matter was hushed and buried. Disgusted at the brutality I witnessed here, I packed up the few articles I had, and resolved to look for a situation somewhere else. At this time I had neither hat on my head, nor shoes to my feet. My whole wardrobe consisted of a Guernsey frock, a pair of trowsers, and a spare shirt, wrapped up in a handkerchief, with some other trifles. Before leaving the town, I resolved to call on my friend the store-keeper. I mounted the steps that led to the piazza of his shop; but seeing him engaged with some gentlemen within, I waited outside of the door till I should see him at leisure. I was still pale and emaciated, in consequence of the fever. He cast his eye on me, and, I dare say, he thought I was dying. He came to the door: the horizon of his countenance was darkened with a most ungracious frown. Surely I came in an unlucky hour. Why did I not wait till the gentleman had taken dinner, and blunted the stings of his spleen in a generous bumper!

"What is it you want with me?" said he, " Go: what should you do here? You can have no claims on me."

I certainly was not prepared for this. He had, unsolicited, promised me his interest and utmost endeavours to procure me a situation, for which I thought myself not unqualified. He had caused me to hang on that promise till my last dollar was expended;—and to receive me thus! It went heavily to my almost hopeless heart; but I was yet more angry than grieved. I thought how I had come from the same country—the same vessel had wafted us across the ocean. I was almost the only survivor of that ship's crew, and now I was desolate in a foreign land, and without bread. I thought on all this, and, but for scorn, I could have wept. Pride, however, lent me all its aid. I bestowed on him a look of contempt, and, without any other answer, proceeded on my journey.

When I had reached the outskirts of the town, I stopped to inquire the direct road to the next sea-port. A gentleman, standing under the piazza of a merchant's store, chancing to observe me, called in a familiar manner—" Ho, Jack, whither are you bound?"—" For Montego Bay, Sir, in search of a ship," was the reply. He then inquired what vessel I belonged to last: I told him. " Oh," cried he, " you are one of Captain F——'s boys. Poor fellow, I knew Captain F——, he was a dear friend of mine. And, what, after undergoing such hardships in their service, have the company turned you adrift?" I told him they had not, but stated my reasons for quitting their service. " You was right," said he, " come along with me, and I'll find you a vessel. I am master of the finest ship in the island, but she is now lying at Lucea." He then took me down to the wharf, and hailing an English ship lying at anchor, a boat came ashore. He requested the people of the boat to take me on board their ship, and to tell their captain, that I was to remain there till his boat should arrive to take me down to Lucea. This was all transacted in the course of a few minutes. I remained some days on board the English ship, whose crew were very kind to me, and expressed a warm wish that I would stop with their own captain, as he wanted a few hands; but I tenaciously stuck to my first patron, and set sail for Lucea in a drugger, being too impatient to wait the arrival of the long-boat. On our way to Lucea we put into Montego Bay, where I lodged a night in the house of my good nurse. Next day I called on a young gentleman, who had been one of our passengers from Greenock. He was now employed in a store as clerk. He treated me with much kindness, and promised to do his utmost to obtain a situation for me. As soon as he could effect this, he would let me know by letter. Before I embarked for Lucea, I called on Messrs. H. and Co., the owners of the vessel in which I left Scotland. They had never paid me the wages due for my servitude. Mr. H—— treated me with great insolence, and told me he would give me nothing, because I had deserted the vessel. Now, the vessel was wrecked, but had been got up again; and although, on recovering from the fever, I had gone on board, I was induced to leave her, along with my friend Phillip, because we understood she was bound for South America, and would not return to Scotland for a number of years. I told Mr. H——, that I had fulfilled my engagement to the very letter and limit of the original contract, and that if he did not pay me, I would use legal measures to compel him. He smiled, and well he might, for he knew that I had not means to put my threat in execution. I was obliged to come away empty, lamenting that I was now in a land where justice—like the gods of some Indian nations—was too exalted to listen to the application of a poor friendless tar.

When I came to Lucea, the master of the drugger put me on board my destined ship—the Cyrus of Whitby. The captain was not on board, but the mate and crew received me with cheerful countenances, telling me, that the captain had intimated to them that such a person was expected. I was taken down to the steerage, where the ship's crew seating themselves in a ring, began to empty two bottles of rum which the mate had sent them, in order to welcome their new shipmate. They drank to my health, and pushed round the glass with boisterous hilarity. When the bumper came to my turn, a person in the far corner of the steerage, on hearing my voice, sprung to his feet, and running towards me, exclaimed—" Is it you' Campbell?" He then clasped me to his bosom, and burst into tears. It was my old shipmate, Phillip Gray. He then related to me all the trying adventures he had passed through since our parting, and expressed his happiness in meeting me again under such agreeable circumstances; for, he told me, he was at present second mate of the ship, and in the event of the first mate obtaining the command of another vessel (an event daily expected), he had the promise of being promoted to his station. He then related to the whole assembled crew the many scenes, trials, and perils we had weathered together; after which, every one on board tried to excel in marks and expressions of friendship to me. I was not many days on board, when a letter from my friend at Montego Bay conveyed the agreeable intelligence, that he had procured for me a situation to my wish, on an estate in his own immediate neighbourhood. This was the ultimate object of my ambition, and, after taking an affectionate leave of my friend Phillip, I set out for my new situation without a moment's delay.

On my way from Lucea to Montego Bay I fell in with a poor tar, whom I had formerly seen at a neighbouring sea-port. He had, along with some other persons, deserted from a man-of-war in rather an extraordinary manner; and as the hue and cry had been raised after them through the whole island, he was obliged to skulk from place to place to avoid pursuit, and, perhaps, an ignominious death. He told me his story,—he and several other seamen, who had been impressed into the service, resolved on making their escape from a frigate lying at Port Royal, and effected their design in the following manner:—The captain and some other officers being on shore, all the ship's boats and their crews, except one, were absent. Orders were issued from the quarter-deck to get this boat manned, and proceed to Kingston on some pressing business. As this boat had no fixed hands attached to it, it was manned indiscriminately by such hands as first presented themselves. My present fellow traveller took care to be one of them. A midshipman had charge of the boat—it was now dark—and their orders were to pull direct for Kingston. When the boat was out of the frigate's reach, the person at the helm began to steer in a direction somewhat out of the accustomed tract. The midshipman ordered him to put down the helm. To this mandate the sailor paid no attention. The midshipman then rose from his seat, and struck him. This usage was resented, and the blow returned. The midshipman then drew his cutlass, and offered to cut the sailor down. A serious scuffle ensued. One or two of the hands endeavoured to extricate the midshipman; but the tar who struggled with him appealed to the remainder of the boat's crew who had entered into the conspiracy, and like Casca, exclaimed—" Help, friends, help; now is your time; liberty or death." The conspirators immediately sprung from their oars, and threw the midshipman overboard. The waters closing over him silenced his screams, and he sunk to rise no more. A dreadful pause ensued. They began to reflect on the atrocity of the deed, and their own awful situation. They knew, that if ever they should be taken or recognized by his majesty's government as the authors of this deed, they would be put to death. They, therefore, pulled the boat to the most solitary part of the bay, and took their flight across the mountains.

I knew this story to be true, for it made a great rumour round the coast at the time; but what surprised me was, to see this poor fellow nowise alarmed at his situation; on the contrary, he used to sing as merrily as a thrush, and tell his story to every one that would listen to it. He was going to Great River in search of a ship. I parted with him at a turn of the road the second day of our pilgrimage, and told him the best luck I could wish him was, a hope that I would never meet him in Jamaica again. In this hope, however, I was mistaken; for, half-a-year afterwards, he called on me at C——, where I was then situate, and told me that he had not yet found a ship; for he was no sooner engaged in one, than he was hunted out of it by the d—d man-of-war cruizers. He was as hearty and reckless as ever; and though known to all the merchant ship's crews on the north of the Island, there was not the slightest offer on their part to avail themselves of the government reward, placarded on the corners of every street. The impress of seamen, and the tyranny of the service, had excited in these men a strong sentiment of indignation. I never saw or heard more of this marine Mercutio; but if he escaped from the Island, he was more indebted to good fortune than to his own prudence.

As travelling on foot is very fatiguing under a vertical sun, and as there are no inns on the roads, I was obliged to call at two or three of the planters' houses for refreshment. In this respect the white population of Jamaica are really hospitable; and as every estate keeps an open table, and some a spare bed, for the accommodation of way-farers, the absence of inns is less felt as an inconvenience. At one of these estates I called on an old friend, to whom I had a letter from my acquaintance in Montego Bay. He was in a situation similar to that which I was on my way to occupy. He treated me with great cordiality, made me a present of some shirts and neckcloths, and after a glass or two of rum—for I would not wait dinner—told me he would let me see his wife. He then ordered a Negro to introduce his wife Daphne. The sable fair one entered; she was a great dowdy of a Negro, with a broad face, squat nose, and a mouth of immense longitude. It is customary with the majority of overseers and book-keepers in Jamaica to have a black or Mulatto slave for their mistress, whom they familiarly call their wife; but of all the white men's wives, Daphne was beyond comparison the most *outre*, and ourang-outang like in appearance. My friend considered himself happy in his choice, and I did not choose to arrogate to myself any superiority of taste, by making disagreeable strictures on his standard of beauty.

I reached Montego Bay on the night before new-year's-day, and found my friend, with about half a dozen more young men from Scotland, preparing to celebrate Hogmanay, in honour of the ancient customs of their forefathers. I was made a welcome participator of their festivity, and felt all the agreeable emotions that usually accompany a sudden change from a situation of toil and peril, to one of ease and security. The Negroes enjoy the time from Christmas to new-year's-day as holidays, and the streets were now crowded with splendid processions, or choaked up with crowds of dancers. This is an amusement of which the Negroes are very fond. Their music generally consists of a small drum, or the skull of a horse, which they strike with a stick. The bystanders accompany this uncouth instrument with some favourite tune. In these dances only two perform at once, a male and female. The female generally confines her movements to the modesty of nature; but the male displays what he considers his powers of agility, by performing the most extravagant and hyperbolical saltations, without aiming at any thing like science or art. They take great delight in this exercise, and the most extravagant buffoon is generally the victor in the eyes of the sombre fair ones of Dahomy and Congo. Their processions were really elegant, but, as far as I could learn, they consisted principally of free Negroes. They were well attired in muslins and silks, accompanied with bands of music. They walked arm in arm, males and females. Sometimes a female with a good voice sung a song, and the whole procession joined in the chorus. They carried, at certain intervals, large artificial trees, stuck full of burning tapers. They usually made a halt at the doors of the wealthier inhabitants, and after chanting some stanzas in praise of the occupant, received a gratuity in money.

After two days, having got myself genteelly equipped, I proceeded with a letter of introduction to the overseer of the estate on which I was to be employed. He received me with politeness, but said he could not absolutely engage me without the approbation of the proprietor, who was then on a visit to another of his estates up the country: however, he invited me to remain with him till his arrival, as he had no doubt but he would come into his own views at once. To hasten the business, he would write to the proprietor, stating that I had just arrived. I accordingly waited, and in a few days Mr. J—— returned. He sent for me immediately, and after a few questions, engaged me at a salary of £70 per annum, exclusive of board, lodging, and washing. This transaction was no sooner concluded, than Mr. J——, turning round to the overseer, accused him of treating his children disrespectfully in his absence. Some high words passed, the overseer threw up his office, and in less than an hour took his departure from the premises. There were now left just one white person on the estate besides myself. This was a young gentleman from Ireland, to whom Mr. J—— offered the management of the concern; but the former declined it, alleging as an excuse, that he intended to quit the Island in the course of a few months. However, he would undertake to superintend the estate till such time as Mr. J—— could provide another overseer. In about two weeks a Mr. D—— took the management. He was a gentleman of respectability, and possessed a considerable coffee estate in the Island; but the coffee market having suffered an unprecedented depression at this time, he undertook the management of the estate, on the stipulated condition of getting fifty of his slaves employed on it, at five shillings currency per diem. This gentleman, being a person of liberal spirit and independant fortune, treated me with great kindness. Under such a master, my mind felt itself in perfect ease and security—free from all those fears and jealousies to which many young men in that country are continually subjected, by the capricious and domineering spirit of some puny tyrant. He kept a good substantial table, which was at all times open to his numerous friends, who were generally men of property and respectability. My duty here was rather an amusement than a labour: when the crop season was at an end I had almost nothing to do, for all the field duty devolved on the other two book-keepers, and Mr. D—— left me at perfect liberty to follow the bent of my own inclination. I was mostly occupied in traversing the grounds, visiting the hospital, and the stations of the different watchmen, and getting our garden put in order. This consisted of a piece of ground finely shaded with tamarind and mangrove trees, oranges, guavas, the breadfruit, and several other tropical plants: also large cocoa-nut trees, and a hedge of bamboos. A fine stream, that drove our sugar-mill, traversed part of this garden, and in its course formed a fine waterfall. Here I used to pass much

of my time, either reading, or watching the labours of a band of fine Negr
children, who, under the guidance of an aged woman, laid it out into see
plots and other various uses. I found this situation, in almost every respect
equal to my wishes. My employer always treated me with kindness an
affection, and, shortly after his accession, advanced my salary; besides, h
procured me credit with his own merchants for my most extensive necessitie:
This I could have obtained almost to any amount, but I made no impruden
use of his generosity; I was, therefore, enabled to leave the Island clear o
debt. Upon the whole, this was, perhaps, the most agreeable period of m
whole life. I lived in ease, content, and affluence, and had the happiness t
acquire the esteem and friendship of a very respectable circle of acquaintance.

When a stranger from the north of Europe arrives at the West Indies, th
first thing that strikes his eye is the deep unvaried verdure of the woods
Here is no withering of leaves—none of that varying assemblage of mellow
tints which, in the autumnal seasons, characterise a northern landscape. Thi
deep green forms a fine contrast with the white sandy beach, and the light
dazzling appearance of the painted towns. On a closer inspection, he is sur
prised to find that he cannot recognise a single shrub or tree, even a blade c
grass. Great part of the animal creation is entirely new to him. The ma
jority of the inhabitants are black—some dressed in tawdry rags, others almos
naked. The heaven is one clear and bright expanse, unblotted with a cloud
Birds and insects of the most exquisite plumage and colours arrest the won
dering eye. The trees are everywhere in unfading bloom—some bearin
fruit, others flowers. There is no fall of the leaf, no cold, no winter; Natur
is in eternal bloom. Some people are planting, when others are reaping. T
the eye of an European, the country has the appearance of a new world.

The Island of Jamaica is mountainous and woody. The blue mountain
have an elevation of 7000 feet above the level of the ocean, and assume
sublime and imposing aspect to ships approaching from the east. The hill
are often isolated; sometimes the disruption of continuity in the land form
deep ravines and gullies, which form the beds of torrents; in other places i
spreads out into fine undulating plains. The country is well watered witl
streams, on the banks of which are situated the houses of planters, with thei
extensive sugar-works, and villages of Negro huts, all studded, and sometime
overshaded with cocoa-nut trees. The fields are everywhere covered with
canes, and the mountains shaded with walks of plantain and banana trees.

The white population of the Island consists principally of adventurers from
Britain. As these never marry, they leave no legitimate offspring behind
them. Almost every white man, however, cohabits with a black slave. The
offspring of these amours are the property of the slave's master. It is hi

interest to encourage the practice; for a West Indian planter estimates his wealth by the number of his slaves, as a shepherd in other countries does by that of his flocks. At the birth of every infant, the mother receives from her master the customary present of a bottle of rum, a calabash of sugar, and a tallow candle. It makes no difference in this respect whether the father of the child be married, or unmarried; the woman's own husband, or a white man.

The slavish condition of the Negroes, and the total absence of moral and religious instruction, is a sufficient excuse for their ignorance. They know nothing about religion, and yet they have more piety than their masters. They are not so deficient in intellectual energy, as is sometimes asserted. A West Indian slave is every whit as rational a creature as a Scots peasant or mechanic, and tinged with less vulgarity. I have conversed with slaves who could reason on right and wrong with as much, and sometimes more good sense than some philosophers—slaves who were conscious of the birth-right of human nature, and eyed their own degradation with just but silent indignation. They are often, it is true, expert in stealing from their masters; but I have heard them maintain with much freedom and boldness, that this was no crime; "Who planted the cane?" said a slave to me one day, when I checked him for abstracting a lump of sugar: "Who nourished its growth? was it not the poor Negro? Negro man work all day in the hot sun; he toil through mud and rain. He have hunger and wet all day, cold all night, yet he plant the cane, he watch over him, he cut him down, carry him to the mill, he make sugar. Shall Buckra man, who do nothing, at all; and poor Negro man, who do all dem tings, starve?" This was logic that might put a tyrant to the blush; yet nothing is more common than to see a Negro extended on the ground by the hands of four strong men, and a hideous cart whip applied to his bare posteriors, for attempting to satisfy his hunger with the puniest portion of the produce of his own labour and skill. Set the most expert white man in Jamaica to boil sugar, I venture to say he will completely spoil it; yet the poor Negro, whose ingenuity and experience directs and executes the manufacture of it, can scarcely procure an ounce of the material to sweeten his coffee. As to rum, he tastes none, except what he may purchase with the money he earns on Sunday at market, with the produce of his provision ground.

The slaves are summoned to labour before sunrise by the sound of a conque shell, or the crack of the cart whip. They work all day in the field almost naked, under a vertical sun. They have one half hour allowed them for breakfast, which they take on the field, and an hour and a half for dinner. Their provision is all of their own rearing, except seven salt herrings on Sunday, which is all the sustenance they receive from the hand of their master. In order to cultivate their provision grounds, they had every second Saturday at their own command. Besides herrings, their proprietors furnish them with a suit of coarse clothes every year, a knife, and a bonnet.

To give a detailed relation of the treatment these unfortunate beings experience from their masters, would shock the feelings of every person whom custom and daily occurrence had not rendered, in some degree, callous to the barbarous practice. I have seen females of a slender form, and handsome in every external grace, thrown down in the face of heaven, and at noonday, before crowds of spectators, to undergo the punishment of the cart whip. Even the parents, or the children of the sufferers, have been present on these occasions. Nay, I have seen old women, tottering on the brink of the grave, used in this manner, in presence of their own offspring. Thirty-nine lashes is the utmost extent to which a master can punish his slave by law; but, thirty-nine lashes with a cart whip! and of more than ordinary dimensions! applied to a female too, and by a European, a native of the land of learning and knight-errantry—blush England! thou art free, and under the mild influences of a gospel dispensation, yet there was nothing in the heathen world, nothing in ancient Egypt or Persia to equal this; and in all Mahomed's dominions there is not at this day a parallel to it. At every stroke of this dreadful instrument of torture, the flesh is ploughed up in furrows, and the screams and writhings of the agonised victim are truly distressing and appalling. My friend Mr. Welsh, who was my fellow-servant on the estate of C——, related to me, that when he was book-keeper on the estate of Paisley, in St. James' parish, his overseer, a man of the name of Morgan, had punished an old female slave with thirty-nine lashes of the cart whip. She was then, according to custom, ordered to the Estate's hospital. After remaining there a few days, her wounds not having been properly dressed, she left the hospital of her own accord, and came to the overseer's house in search of the doctor, whose arrival there had been certified to her by some friendly slave; for a doctor in the interior has to attend several estates. The doctor, the overseer, and my friend, were walking under the piazza when the poor old woman approached them. The overseer, on hearing her complaint, burst into a fit of laughter. " O," says he to the doctor, " leave her to me, I will soon cure her." Previous to this, the doctor and he had examined her wounds, and found they were what is commonly called fly-blown. Morgan then called for some gunpowder, and making it into a paste, ordered a slave to rub it into her sores. This being done, he called for a match, and lighting it with a segar, set fire to the wetted powder. The poor woman was then wrapped in a blaze of fire, and her screams and agonies were no doubt violent. Th doctor and my friend had done all in their power to prevent Morgan from putting his diabolical cure in practice, but their entreaties had no effect. Next day the poor old woman died, in consequence of undergoing such a fiery ordeal; but Morgan suffered no other punishment (although an information was laid before the Custos of St. James' parish by my friend Mr. Welsh) than an immediate dismissal from his situation. Mr. Welsh, instead of receiving the thanks of the proprietors of the Paisley estate for this laudable service, was also cashiered.

Prior to the abolition of the slave trade, the planters used their Negroes as we do stage-coach horses in this country, they wrought or drove them so hard, that in two or three years they were past service, and then abandoned them to hunger and disease. Mr. Dodd, my overseer, used to give me some curious anecdotes of the treatment of Negroes in Jamaica when he was a young man, and newly come to the Island. At this time he had been thirty years in the country. Among others he told me,—that there was an old woman, a Negro, on the estate of Dundee, who, being superannuated, went about at her pleasure. The overseer, of course, thought her existence a tax on the industry of his other slaves, and, wishing to get rid of her entirely, ordered the slave drivers to carry her up to the top of a hill, and pitch her down into a gully, or natural cauldron, formed by a sudden turn of the river, at the base of an acclivitous precipice. The poor Negroes, more humane than their master, wished to evade the stern decree, by removing the old dame to a place of concealment. This passed for some time; but the poor woman, impatient of restraint, sallied out from her retreat, and, unfortunately, the first person she met was her old tyrant, the Dionysius of Dundee. He was this time resolved not to be outwitted, and calling the drivers again to his assistance, ordered them to carry her to the top of the precipice, and, accompanying them in person, he saw them plunge her into the horrid gulf. The old Circe, however, by some lucky intervention of providence, made her escape from the watery element, and effected her way home. A few days afterwards she sallied out once more on a ramble among the rocks, and just as she was doubling the rugged angle of one of them, met Busha again right in the teeth. He imagined, no doubt, that she was now an inhabitant of another world, and found himself, by some spell of horror, cast into a cold sweat. The old woman eyed him with a ghastly grin, and muttering something like a curse, disappeared among the thick bushes. Busha, for that is the name the Negroes give an overseer, trembled in lith and limb, and making all the speed homeward he could, went to his bed, sent for the doctor, took medicine, and died.

The Negroes, when I was in Jamaica, had no access to literary or religious instruction. Those born in the Island professed Christianity, yet their masters did not offer them even the means of regular baptism. The truth is, the masters for the most part have less Christianity in their conduct and profession than the slaves they govern. Infidelity among them is a creed of very extensive acceptation. Even born Jews in Jamaica are many of them what is called free-thinkers. Young gentlemen from this country may be very pious believers on their arrival there, but, like sheep, they are soon infected with the moral plague of the country; and after a few years they divest their consciences of all religious restraint, and walk triumphantly under the apostolic banners of Hume and Voltaire. They are strangers to the endearing appellations of parent and child, wife and husband, and all the other ties and tendrils of relationship which bind the families of the old world to each other.

I was at length seized with an obstinate quotidian ague, which I combated at first with apparent success; but three successive relapses reduced me to a state of extreme debility, and, finally, obliged me to adopt the resolution of leaving the Island. I, therefore, after long hesitation, took farewell of a country in which, notwithstanding all its faults, I might be said to have left the half of my heart. In the latter end of 1814, I accordingly took my passage on board a vessel bound for London. As I recovered my health immediately on coming to sea, I intended returning again to the Island, and the captain of the ship in which I embarked kindly offered to give me a free passage back again. There was also a West Indian planter a passenger in the same ship, who was an intimate friend of Mr. Dodds, my former overseer. He not only encouraged me to return, but promised, by his interest and influence, to get me engaged in one of the most respectable houses in the island. All this was very flattering, and, as I had fully recovered from the effects of my ague, I meant to avail myself of the disinterested patronage of these gentlemen; but as a period of three or four months would elapse before the captain's ship could be ready for sea after her arrival at London, I thought it advisable in the meantime to proceed to Scotland. The words *home* and *native land* had charms in them which my heart could not resist, and I accordingly took my passage from London to Leith, and once more set my foot on the idolized land of valour and song. On my arrival, I found the family all well, but little expecting my return. It was the dusk of the evening when I arrived at my mother's house: I rapped at the door—a girl opened. I found the old woman sitting by the fire spinning at her wheel, and humming a Gælic song which she had composed herself, and of which I was the subject; she bewailed the absence of her son. I walked up to her, and inquired if this was the house in which such a person dwelt. She stopped her wheel, and good naturedly answered, "this is the house." I kept conversing with her for some moments to amuse myself, when, suddenly recognising me, she sprung from her wheel, and bursting into tears, grasped me in her arms. She had previously received a false report of my death. The suddenness and reality of this contradiction made her quite happy.

Shortly after this, I called on one of my old friends at Glasgow, who had once been a conspicuous member of our village club. He had now completed a course of University education, and possessed, for the time being, a lecturer's chair. He advised me, instead of returning to the West Indies, to come to Glasgow, and study medicine. Such an acquirement would enable me to earn a livelihood in whatever quarter of the world fortune should place me, and, at the same time, would be more in unison with a love of literary pursuits, than any situation connected with the West Indies, or mercantile affairs. I followed his advice; and after attending a course of very instructive lectures in his own class, commenced next season the study of anatomy and chemistry, under the auspices of Doctors Jeffray and Thomson, in the University of Glasgow. During this progress his friendship was of peculiar advantage to me, and afforded me many facilities, of which I would have otherwise been deprived.

On quitting the University, and finding myself in rather a state of pecuniary embarrassment, I began to practice medicine in a small village in the West Highlands. The situation, indeed, was rather an unlucky one, for the district was poor and healthy. I had, notwithstanding a good deal of practice, but money was as scarce as the philosopher's stone. The country was but thinly peopled, and the visits were frequently to a great distance, among bleak and heathy hills, where the fatigue was long and laborious, and the prospect of remuneration often uncertain. I was tired of toiling for nothing, and seeing my days stealing away like a shadow, without any prospect of independence, I therefore quitted the scene, and in order to refit myself for some more congenial situation, I betook myself to manual labour, hoping, by hard toil and economy, I would be enabled to amass a sum of money that would convey me across the Atlantic, where most of my relations reside. Our day dreams are often as fallacious as those that float on the pillow of sleep. Pope says—

" Man never is but always to be blest;"

and this was exactly my case. I could never attain to the desired sum; but it was a favour that hope held out to the heart, like the expectation of an estate in chancery. Thus, like Ixion, I still turned the wheel, hoping that the spoke now in the nadir would soon mount to the zenith.

I was once more in Glasgow, and employed as a spinner, in which capacity I earned about thirty shillings per week. It was here I formed an acquaintance with one whom I loved, which proved unfortunate to us both, as it ended in her death, and my misery.

All my misfortunes and little disappointments were nothing previous to this calamity. I could have looked on my past life with a meek and unrepining spirit, and moved on in the noiseless tenor of my pilgrimage with, at least, a kind of negative contentment, but this fatal—this unsuspected catastrophe has overcome me, like the malignant mist of the Lego whose vapour was death—there was a kind of feeling in all my former struggles with misfortune that had a taste of virtue, and even of glory in it, but that feeling has here forsaken me. I find myself plunged into the most dreadful of human errors, and rendered the victim of a sorrow that neither time nor repentance can wear away. My greatest, perhaps my sole consolation, is, that the fatal deed was committed at a time when my intellectual powers were wraped by an insane imagination, and in a state of phrenzy over which reason had no control. Whatever, therefore, my sorrow may be, however poignant or incurable, I have the inward consolation to feel that Heaven has not poisoned my cup with the bitter ingredient of remorse. The deed could not be one of hatred or revenge, for the victim of it was, at the time, of all human creatures the most dear to me ; the evidence produced at my trial, and the verdict of a jury founded on that evidence, go clearly to prove that the deed was committed when my mind was subject to an insane delusion, but upon these grounds I do not wish to rest my justification, I look upward to that tribunal where there is no extenuation of guilt, no overshadowing of innocense, and I bow before it with humility and hope. My cause is in the hands of the Eternal: I know that my trial is yet to come on, I am, therefore, little concerned about human opinion, whether it be for or against me. Man may punish my body, but God alone can reach my conscience ; and I rejoice that his forbearance has hitherto been that of a merciful parent, and that he has secretly strengthened me with the spirit of hope and peace.

My connection with this unfortunate female, although, perhaps, not the result of absolute wisdom, was at least sanctioned by the sincerest and most honourable of motives; if it should be averred by some, that the step was an imprudent one, I have only to answer, that Love seldom views his object through a microscope. There are situations and circumstances in which the best, if not the wisest of men, are carried out of the right forward path of worldly prudence by this noble passion of our frame, miscalled a weakness of the heart, because it sometimes leads astray, but if it be a weakness, it is an amiable one, which always awakes the sympathy of our nature, and often excites more interest than the Stoic's virtue. Lord Shaftsbury somewhere says " That it is not the want of knowledge, but a perversion of the will, that fills men's actions with folly, and their lives with disorder." This excellent maxim will undoubtedly hold true in all cases where the moral business of life is concerned——except in love.

Omnia vincit amor et nos cedamus amori.

The greatest moral pilots of the world have, some of them, impinged on that rock, not from any perversion of the will, but because they were carried away by an irresistible impulse of nature, which philosophy may deride, but can seldom curb or vanquish. I must, therefore, bewail the event, but it would be fruitless to reflect on the cause which impelled me, with a power like Omnipotence, into a measure so unhappy in its result. The graver part of my acquaintance might look upon it as a departure from prudence, but I was too deeply engaged to listen to any retrograde suggestion, and had the matter been let alone, had it roused no malignant speculation, had friends and foes not poured in their heterogeneous potion of advice and scandal, the consequences would not, in my own opinion, have proved unhappy. She was young, handsome, of a pliable disposition, and in spite of the suggestions and inuendoes of the rigidly righteous, might have turned out a better example of virtue than her detractors.

Shortly after this event, I began to grow melancholy, and from an incessant brooding on what I deemed the hardship of my condition, became the victim of disordered imagination. Without being able to assign any adequate cause, I forsook a profitable employment, and for some time, wandered about in a state of absolute insanity. I was so overpowered with an apprehension that people were coming to murder me in my bed, that I could not sleep two nights in the same house. In this state, I committed many awkward things, and was tortured by a thousand insane phantasies. I would not venture to return home at night without two or three friends to escort me, and even when thus provided and conducted to the very door of my lodgings, the apprehension would suddenly seize me, that some ruffians were concealed under my bed. With a sudden bound I would then spring away from them, and in order to elude their pursuit, break into some garden or field, leap over fences, or whatever obstruction lay in my way, and fly to some distant quarter for shelter. Sometimes filled with the melancholy idea that my best friends were in a conspiracy to take my life, I have passed the whole night on the streets, or in the fields. I once fancied that three men, when I was quitting a house, leapt down upon me from the roof, and pursued me a great way into the country. Were I not now convinced of the insane delusion of my ideas at that time, I would still feel convinced of the reality of this terrible deception, for I not only saw them with clubs pursuing me, but they were sometimes within touch of me. I entered a house where I thought I would find protection, and even after the most solemn assurance on the part of the people of the house, that no harm would reach me, I could not rest satisfied, but rushed out again, and travelled in the dark over hedges, ditches and bye-ways, till I found myself more than twenty miles from Glasgow. I was filled with a strong impression that my enemy was going to assassinate me, and in order to self-defence, I generally carried a knife, hammer, or some other deadly weapon.

After three months from the commencement of this disorder I began to get more composed in mind; the horrible idea of assassination subsiding, I now once more returned to my work, and continued for a short time pretty steadily; but my old paroxysms returning with increased exacerbation of symptoms, I became incapable of continued attendance, and my employer at length intimated to me, that he was under the necessity of substituting another man in my place. I was now desirous of quitting the country, and lament that my friends made no efforts to indulge me in this propensity, as it would have effectually prevented the tragic scene that ensued.

Of that scene I will not attempt a description.—Indeed, I am incapable of giving any from personal experience. I have but a confused remembrance of some parts of it, and for a clear knowledge of the whole transaction, I am as much indebted to the evidence adduced in the annexed trial, as any of my readers can be. All I recollect, is, that I entered the house in which the event took place some time about ten o'clock on the night of the *5th* December, 1825, and that I saw John Orr, who introduced me into a room where there was music and dancing. When rising to dance, I was surprised to find Sarah M'Vicar fronting me in the reel. John Orr subsequent told me, that he and a Mrs. Salmon, a woman of his acquaintance, had brought her there, having gone to her lodgings for that purpose, and persuaded her to accompany them, when she was undressing to go to bed. He then communicated to me by way of secrecy, some facts of a revolting description, which he said had taken place that night, previous to their arrival at the house in which we then were. As he made solemn asseverations to the truth of what he related, I implicitly believed his account, and the thought of it at the time inflamed me to a pitch of indescribable phrenzy. I remember being in company with him and others subsequent to this information, but have no clear recollections of what ensued, or in what manner I was conducted to the Police Office, where I found myself stretched or rather seated on a bench about day-break next morning. I had just waked from a sound sleep, and on turning round my eyes, saw Mrs. Salmon sitting opposite to me by the fire. She told that Sarah was dead. I was struck with this intelligence, as by a shock from heaven, and I could not but bitterly bewail the fatality that caused me to stumble, the preceding evening, on such a scene, and into company whose language and conduct provoked me to such extremity, and who scarcely seem to have made a single effort to restrain me, when they must have been aware, from my conduct and appearance, that I was bent on something frantic.

I have had time enough, and inclination too, to examine myself on the subject of this night's catastrophe. I have dwelt on it in every possible variety of light and shade, but the feeling uppermost in my heart at the end of every examination has been, a mingled one of sorrow and wonder, such a feeling as one might be supposed to entertain on contemplating the devastations of an avalanche or earthquake. I have been told that the work was mine, and all its bitter consequences have overwhelmed me, not with a momentary grief, but one written in an indelible, but inexplicable hieroglyphic. I have shuddered to think the deed was mine, but when the accusing spirit passed, it frowned not on me; for I could find nothing in the composition of my heart to recognize so horrid a principle.

In taking a retrospect of the events of my past life, I find that, with the best intentions in the world, I have been often disappointed in my favourite pursuits, and rendered peculiarly the victim or sport of a capricious fortune. I felt my mind endowed with a natural buoyancy, that gave a sanguine tinge to my hopes, under the very worst of circumstances, and made me look with an air of indifference on almost all the little crosses and downfalls that marked my humble lot. I was always an admirer of a maxim of Seneca's:—" That a virtuous man, struggling to raise himself superior to his misfortunes, was a scene in the human drama, calculated to excite the admiration of the gods." In the same spirit, I have often consoled myself with the fact, that, though my utmost efforts to render myself independent were finally ineffectual, the means I embraced were always honourable, and consistent with the strictest rules of virtue. Fortune, therefore, though she sometimes precipitated me from my little elevations, and threw a cloud over my fondest hopes, could never thoroughly break my heart : as the goddess seemed lavish of her frowns I used to contemplate her favours with a kind of proud apathy, and appreciate them with a glance similar to what, in treading the autumnal forest, we cast on the withered leaves. There is a point of view in which the humblest of mankind may contemplate his own situation with calm complacency, and smile at the superiority which his more fortunate brethren of the human race enjoy. He may do this with safety, and without arrogating to himself any large share of wisdom, when he reflects on his own immortality, and the fleeting and perishing nature of those advantages in the proud possession of others, and the lack of which is, perhaps, the only consideration that lowers him in the scale of human estimation. Better for a man to look with contempt on the enjoyments he cannot obtain, than sit down like Niobe all tears, and repine at the dispensations of Providence. I am now a prisoner without any certain hope of release, and my heart strings have been torn asunder by a calamity the most lamentable that could befall a human being, yet I still, in a great measure, cherish the same cast of feeling. Since my imprisonment, the little circle of my mother's family has been totally broken up, and herself laid in the grave. I have thus been deprived of the assistance that used to be tendered me by my nearest relatives, and, in effect, despoiled of almost every earthly comfort; yet, I do not repine. If God has judged it meet to lay his hand heavily upon me, shall I tax him with injustice? or if he has forborne wholly to cut me off, should I, by falling into a heartless despair, destroy myself? I am too much awake to my responsibility as a rational and immortal being to answer these questions in the affirmative. Though my lot has been one of bitter and blightening misfortune, I have a lively impression that heaven has dealt mercifully with me, and I bow to the irresistible fiat of Omnipotence. The chart of my destiny is before him, and it may be, that his finger has traced on it an outlet, an unseen channel of deliverance, from the rocks and reefs with which my bark seems now surrounded :—Hope

Cheers us through life, nor quits us when we die.

Were I so situated as to be able to do myself and others a benefit, and to take exercise in the open air, I would scarcely envy the world the superiority of its privileges. I am now upwards of two years in prison, and during that period, I may say, the breeze has not fanned my cheek; but, in all other respects, my situation has been as comfortable as the humanity of the Governor could possibly render it. The apartment in which I lodge is the most comfortable in the house, being the only one in which there is a fire, and tolerable company. I am also indebted to the Magistrates for their kindness in giving cash in place of my allowance of food, a measure which has been of incalculable benefit to me; for, though the amount is but triffling, it enables me to come at some indispensable necessaries of which (now that my relations are gone) I would otherwise have had to indure a total privation.

Being now about to close this sketch, I think it incumbent on me to mention my obligations to Mr. Neil Snodgrass, of Mile-End, a gentleman not more distinguished for the ingenuity and usefulness of his numerous inventions in machinery, connected with Cotton Spinning, than beloved by all who know him for a characteristic generosity of spirit. The deep interest he took in my case—his solicitude in finding for me able counsel at my trial—and afterwards the generous, though unsuccessful attempts he made to obtain my liberation have, altogether, founded a claim on my gratitude, that may be conceived, but which I am at a loss to find language to express. My sincere and grateful thanks are also due to an extensive circle of friends and acquaintances, both in town and country, for the generous aid they lent me on the above occasion. I am sorry that cruel necessity has fettered the demonstrations of my gratitude to a bare acknowledgment, and that, as I am at present situated, I can make no better return.

TRIAL

OF

CHARLES CAMPBELL,

BEFORE THE

CIRCUIT COURT OF JUSTICIARY,

At Glasgow, 27th April, 1826.

TRIAL.

After the jury was impannelled, Mr. Russel, counsel for the prisoner, informed the Court that the line of defence which he intended to adopt, was to prove the unfortunate man at the bar to be insane when he committed the horrid deed with which he stood charged.

The Sheriff-Depute for Lanarkshire and Sheriff-Substitute proved the authenticity of the prisoner's declaration, and of his being in a perfectly sane state of mind when he emitted it.

Jean Paton was in Johnson's public-house on 5th Dec. last, with John Orr, and the wife of pannel; left Johnson's, and went to M'Gown's public-house; found a great company there; there was a dance; Mrs. Campbell (pannel's wife) danced; knows the prisoner; danced a reel with him; the couple who faced them was John Orr and Mrs. Campbell; heard Campbell say to his wife, " are you there, Sarah ?" Afterwards Daniel Orr took Mrs. Campbell out of the room; witness went also; Campbell came into the room; Mrs. C. was sitting on the same chair with Orr; did not hear Campbell challenge his wife; heard Mrs. C. say that pannel had no right to her; saw Campbell attempt to strike her; did not know with what sort of instrument; it had a clear shining light; Daniel Orr pushed him back, and prevented the blow. Witness after this went into the kitchen; returned in a little and asked Mrs. C. out of the company; her reason for so doing was, that she thought there might be a disturbance on account of Mrs. C. giving pannel insolence—calling him *daft*—always said he was *daft*. Mrs. C. however did not leave the room with her. About an hour afterwards, saw Mrs. C. come out of the room; saw blood flowing from her; heard her say she was much pained; Dr. Callaghan came and dressed the wound; Mrs. C. said to her, " Don't hold my hands;" heard her say no more; died immediately after that. Saw Campbell in the room after she was dead; heard him say nothing.—Cross-examined.—When in Johnson's public-house warned Mrs. Campbell to leave Orr's company, because she thought he was a bad man. During the reel which she had in M'Gown's, when Mrs. C. was at same time on the floor, heard the latter say to Orr, her partner, " Hang you, Orr, give me a good *swing*." Daniel Orr was sitting with his arms about Mrs. C.'s neck in the back-room. When in Johnson's, heard John Orr say to Mrs. C., " You are the wife of Charles Campbell ;" to which she replied, that she was not, and said, as a reason, " who would take a daft

E

man ?"—(By Lord Meadowbank.)—Knew prisoner one year; he was a cotton-spinner, and was some time out of employment. He practised as a surgeon; got some practice; did not know him afterwards to return to cotton-spinning; could not say that his conduct was any thing else than that of a sane man; saw nothing particular in his manner on the night of the unfortunate occurrence; when he came into the dancing-room, he spoke to no one farther than asking a drink of cold water, and soliciting to dance; said nothing to him during the reel; did not see ORR kiss Mrs. C. when in the back-room.—(By a Juryman.) Pannel and his wife were living separately at this time.

DANIEL ORR remembers being in M'Gown's on 5th Dec., when there was a dance; saw the prisoner there; saw also Mrs. Campbell, who came in with John Orr; Mrs. C. danced with John, and also with himself; did not see pannel dance, being himself worse of liquor; went out with Mrs. C. and Daniel Sutherland into a back-room; saw pannel come in shortly after. Mrs. C. sat between him and Sutherland; when pannel came in, Mrs. C. sprang from her seat towards the window; pannel said he bought her the rings which were in her ears; on this Mrs. C. struck pannel, and threw her arms about witness's neck and kissed him; said she was not prisoner's wife; does not know what pannel did when she kissed him. Mrs. C. expressed a fear that pannel was going to murder her. Prisoner rose and made a blow at her across the table; witness kept him off, and drove him back to his seat; heard Mrs. C. say that pannel was going to stab her; saw nothing in pannel's hands. Some time after, prisoner made a second blow at her; saw blood coming from her neck; heard Mrs. C. cry she was stabbed, and call for a doctor; he went and brought one, and when he came back found the police in the house. After pannel had done the deed, he resumed his seat; thought pannel was not in the possession of his right mind; reason for so thinking was, that he sat down so composed and collected. Knew pannel for some time before; could not say he ever saw any thing peculiar in his manner previous to this event.

DANIEL SUTHERLAND recollects being in M'Gown's house on the night in question, when there was a dance; saw Mrs. C. dance with John Orr, and the prisoner on the floor at same time; saw a disinclination on the part of Mrs. C. to set to pannel in the reel. Witness went into the back-room with Mrs. C. when pannel came in. Mrs. C. was sitting beside Daniel Orr; saw no liberties used with her at that time; heard pannel ask Mrs. C. if she was not his lawful wife, when she answered him no; pannel attempted to strike her, but was prevented; saw a knife in his hand, but could not identify it; saw him make a thrust at her a second time; Mrs. C. cried murder! saw blood coming from her bosom; knew pannel for only two months previous; saw nothing in pannel's manner that made him believe he was insane; only at times, in the course of his acquaintance, thought he was silly; his reason for so thinking was, that he talked about his medical cures, and said he could dye hair to any colour; this was all his reason for thinking he was silly. (Cross-examined.) Mrs. C. was sitting between witness and Daniel Orr when the first blow was given; a quarter of an hour elapsed between the first and second blow; could recollect no other reason than what he had now stated, for thinking pannel was silly.

WILLIAM ROWAN saw pannel come into the back-room already mentioned, and sit down; said to Mrs. C., "My dear, are you here?" and "Are you not my wife?" to which she answered in the negative. Heard something said about ear-rings, and Mrs. C. call pannel bad names; saw him rise, but did not see him strike Mrs. C.; he heard her cry, "Keep him off me; did not see a blow given, his back being turned at the time, but when he looked round, he saw Mrs. C.'s hand at her neck, and crying for a doctor; saw blood flowing; saw the prisoner at this time in the act of sitting down; pannel held something clear in his hand; did not hear any one challenge pannel for the deed; saw him lift his hat, and then fall to the ground; thinks prisoner had been drinking that night; saw no kissing going on between Daniel Orr and the deceased.

ROBT. LACHAN was in company with Wm. Rowan in M'Gown's back room on the night in question—saw Mrs. C. come in with Daniel Orr and Sutherland. Prisoner came in afterwards, and said, Sarah, are you not my wife?—I think it would be better looking if you were sitting beside me. She replied he was *daft*, and would have nothing to do with him. Saw pannel start to his feet, with something in both hands—could not say what he held, but it looked clear—went after this into the kitchen—saw the deceased come in there crying for a doctor.

WM. MUIRHEAD said he was in his own house when he heard a disturbance in the street—came down—heard one say *Charlie* Campbell has stabbed Sarah. Saw pannel coming out of M'Gown's door, when he turned him back, saying some one wanted him. Heard pannel say she deserved it all. —(Cross-examined.)—Pannel was walking and not running down the street when he first saw him, made no resistance whatever when he accosted him. —(By Lord Meadowbank.)—Before any body could have got out of the back door of M'Gown's house, he must go through the kitchen—knew pannel before—saw nothing about him that could make him believe he was insane.

CAMPBELL LECKIE, serjeant in the Calton Police, said, when he came to the Police-office on the night in question, he found the pannel there asleep.— About six in the morning he awoke, and asked what news—witness said no news but bad news—You have murdered poor Sarah. Pannel replied, Have I!—I have then murdered her whom I love best in the world—he evinced violent sorrow, and wished he had a dagger to put into his own heart. Cried " O, that villain! O, that villain! Orr!"—Pannel told him that he had been at a dance in M'Gown's house, and that he had seen Sarah there—had tapped her on the cheek, and asked her to come and sit beside him—said he saw Orr sitting beside her, with his hands on her breast—on which he said, " Sally you ought rather to sit beside me"—she replied, " Go away to your wife and family at Johnstone"—when he answered, " You know, Sally, that I told you before we were married, that a woman there had two children by me, but she is not my wife." He said that when in the back-room he made to stab her, but was prevented—" O, why did they not prevent me when I came to give the fatal blow,—but I must suffer for the deed by the laws of my country." Witness could not say that pannel was quite sober.—(Cross-examined.)— Saw pannel tear his hair and strike his forehead with his hands—thought his sorrow real and unaffected. Before he had told him of what he had done, he showed no consciousness of what had happened—he looked up to the roof and cast his eyes wildly around.—(By Lord Meadowbank.)—The impression on his mind was, that he was amazed at the place where he was. Nine months ago he heard him say in a company, I have a society to attend, and must go, perhaps I have only 24 hours to live—did not think he was the worse of liquor when he thus expressed himself. Upon no other occasion did he observe symptoms of madness in his general conduct. Pannel did not say at any time in the Police-office that he had committed the action in a fit of insanity, or accounted for it at all in that way.

Mr. CALLAGHAN surgeon, being sworn, read from his notes, which were taken at the time, that he was called, on the night in question, to the house of M'Gown—that having arrived there he found the deceased laying on the kitchen floor, still breathing, with her upper garments red with blood—that he ordered her to be removed to another room, that the wound might be examined and dressed; that bright arterial blood was flowing in jets from a small wound situated in the neck, on the left side of the sternum; that he ordered a finger to be placed on the wound to stop the bleeding; that very soon afterwards the pulse became imperceptible, the face cadaverous, the lower jaw fell, and she expired. Had no doubt the wound in the neck was the cause of her death. Here the witness wished to read from his paper some observations which he had made on the state of the prisoner, but the Court prevented him. Lord Meadowbank, however, requested him to give him the paper, which was then handed to his Lordship. The examination afterwards continued.

Had known the pannel for sometime previous to the murder; considered his mind to be in a state of alienation; had been consulted by him frequently about diseases, which, upon scrutiny being made, turned out to be imaginary; Campbell had asked him for medicines (the nature of which, however, he could not recollect) which, though not poisonous, were not inapplicable to the disease he imagined himself to labour under, yet he did not feel himself at liberty to give him, as he did not think he needed them.—Saw in his walk and gait something *outre*.—Knew no other reason than the above for thinking him insane.

DR. CORKINDALE was then called. Was ordered by a remit from the sheriff to examine the body of the deceased the day after the murder. Was shown a report which he and Mr. Neilson had made of the case at the time and identified it. He then was requested to read it. It stated that they found on the neck of the deceased, to the left side of the breast-bone, a wound about half-an-inch long, and two inches deep, which was ascertained by introducing a probe; that upon dissecting the neck, the lethal instrument was found to have penetrated to the left subclavian artery, one of the largest arteries in that vicinity, that it was divided to the extent of two thirds of its circumference; that there was about a pound of blood found within the thorax and that they had no doubt death was occasioned by, and very soon followed the infliction of this wound. The Doctor then deponed that he saw Campbell in the Jail two days after the murder, and has seen him there about 1 times since; that then, and afterwards, with every wish and opportunity to ascertain the fact, he considered him to be quite sane.

MR. F. NEILSON corroborated Dr. Corkindale in every particular.

The declaration of the prisoner was then read, and his Counsel afterwards proceeded to examine the exculpatory proof.

George Turnbull, cotton-spinner, was acquainted with prisoner for a long time, and wrought in the same mill and flat with him in April, 1825: saw him often speaking, as it were, to the ceiling; asked him why he talked so; when pannel replied he was conversing with the people in the upper flat; told him he could talk to any body at a great distance; called him once to the window, and asked him to look at the cotton weavers, for they were all come down to murder him; witness saw no weavers; pannel ran out of the mill; witness followed him; he went in the direction of the Green, when pannel discovered him; he appeared afraid, and seemed anxious to escape from him: pannel was in the habit of carrying instruments about him, and gave as a reason for so doing, that he wished to defend himself against the Calton weavers. Witness called upon pannel's friends, and told them that something should be done for him, as it was his opinion he was deranged. Application was made to have him confined in the Lunatic Asylum, but the fees of that Institution were found to be so high, that the measure was abandoned for a time.—(Cross-examined)—Saw pannel some time since April, 1825, and did not think his intellect was much improved; he was frequently off work; there was no combination at that time to cause this; had not been drinking when he was talking foolishly to the roof, or when he supposed people coming to murder him. His master was aware that pannel was subject to such fits, and had instructed him to take him out when so troubled.

Angus Chisholm, cotton-spinner, has known prisoner for two years, and wrought with him on the same flat. Sometimes thought him deranged; for example, asked him once, when he had been off work in April, 1825, where he had been, and was told that he was seeing Mr. Miller, writer, as he understood he was going to be tried at next Circuit Court, and he wished to know from Miller what it was for. One morning he came into the mill, and accused one of the girls for disturbing him in the night time, so that he could get no sleep for her crying through the ceiling to him, and abused her very much for so doing. Pannel often interfered with witness's piecers, and he was afraid to challenge him for it, although he was quite sensible he was innocent of what he laid to his charge. At one time pannel, in witness's presence, told the master to pay him his wages, because he (witness) had dismissed him from the premises. Pannel carried instruments about him, in order to protect himself against the Calton weavers.

James M'Phail, cotton-spinner, deponed that pannel came to his house and asked a bed from him; witness said that he would give him one, if he would be quiet. His reason for saying so was, that he knew him to be mad. He kept quiet for some time, but at once rose out of the bed, and said, " that the Calton weavers were now coming to seize him, but threatened that he would do for them." Witness rose out of bed, and found pannel with a fork in his hand, at the door, which was open. He would not go to rest again until he received a stick and a smoothing iron, which he took to bed with him. Witness had a female who stopped in his house, a friend of his wife's. Pannel accused her of being in league with the weavers outside, and talking to them in the *nob* language—made attempts to punish her for so doing, but was prevented. On another night witness slept with him at pannel's mother's house, but he got up in the night-time, felt the window and door if they were secure, and then laid down again in bed.—(By Lord Meadowbank.)—The house was one stair up, and this took place at eleven o'clock at night. Witness was one of the men, who went to get him into the Lunatic Asylum, this was about the beginning of summer 1825. Witness could not say whether, if pannel was putting a knife into his bosom, that he (the pannel) would have considered he was committing a crime—witness could not say whether, from any thing he heard in the conversation of the prisoner, that he thought murder was a crime. Lord Meadowbank asked witness in a peremptory manner— Would you, Sir, have gone to bed with a person whom you considered did not know stabbing another through the heart was an offence? Witness made no answer.

ANGUS M'PHAIL said prisoner was in his employment—did not think him qualified for doing his work—he observed that he laboured under strong delusions—did not think these were produced by drink, but it appeared to him that he was deranged—earned at times L.4 10s in the fortnight—his mental delusions did prevent him from attending closely to his work; and he employed, during these absences, another spinner in his place, who received for the time he was off work the major part of the L.4 10s.

MARY M'KINLAY went to the prisoner's mother's house—saw the latter put victuals down upon the table—pannel took up the knife which was placed there also, and put it into his pocket—would not give it up to her, for he said he would carry it to defend himself against the weavers—said he would part with any thing to her but the knife—witness was convinced pannel was insane, and carried lines to the Rev. Mr. Turnbull's church, requesting, in his behalf, prayers to be offered up for " a person troubled in body and mind." Saw pannel about three weeks before the 5th December last—did not think him then much better—told her he was going abroad, and no devils would there come near him—never saw the prisoner the worse of liquor.

JOHN MUIR has known the prisoner from his infancy, and lives in Johnstone —the prisoner came out to Johnstone last spring, and asked of him a room and a gill, and said he wished to talk with him—pannel told him that he wanted a pistol, but he replied he had no such thing in his house, and said a pistol was a dangerous thing, and ought not to carry one—pannel then said that he was combined against him like all the world—witness then asked him what he meant to do with a pistol, when he replied he wished to put an end to his existence, and settle this disturbance—pannel called on him a second time in Johnstone on 22d Nov. last, but he would not admit him into any of his rooms because he was afraid of him—pannel told him he was going to take up a medicine shop in Bridgeton—witness then said he would call upon him there when he went to Glasgow. Immediately after that pannel denied having said that he was going to commence such a shop; but stated that he told him he was going to Tarbert, where he was to see him at the salt water—this was said just a few minutes after he made the former statement.

ALEXANDER DOVE.—I saw the prisoner at the Bridge of Weir: we took a walk together, and had some conversation. He told me that he had something to tell me, but was afraid to do so, as he had many enemies in Glasgow, and what he said *here* would be heard *there*. I told him that was impossible, the sound of his voice could not travel so far. He then said, that there was a point of philosophy which he advocated, but which he could get nobody to believe in ; and that if he could get only one respectable convert, things would soon go all his own way. It was, that sound had no limits; that the lowest whisper can be heard at an infinite distance ; and even that if you only *think*, your ideas will be conveyed any where you pleased. I told him, of course, that all this was quite absurd, but he was quite obstinate. He then asked *my* opinion of the limits of sound. I told him its limits depended upon circumstances; particularly, upon the degree of the causes, the sonorousness of the sounding bodies, and the medium through which the sound was transmitted. But I could not get him convinced, and we parted, each with his own opinion.

The learning of this witness, who is a common cotton-mill mechanic in the village of Johnstone, astonished and amused the whole court, particularly Mr. Jeffrey, whom we observed to be much pleased. We may take this opportunity of observing, that in the whole of this trial we were much struck with the talents, intelligence, and decent appearance of the witnesses—men and women collected promiscuously from among the operatives of our cotton-mill population.

ALEX. BARBOUR lives in York-street, and remembers going with pannel to the steam-boat quay. Pannel said he was going down the water. After waiting there for some time, pannel changed his intention, and would not go; asked his reason for so doing, and he said, " Did I not see the villains on board the boat who had entered into a conspiracy against me ;" Pannel asked witness if he thought Mrs. Barbour would do him a favour, which was, to lend him a knife, with which, he said, he would defend himself against the villains who conspired for his life, knowing, as he did, that they were all cowards; if he just showed his weapon, they would not have courage to meddle with him. Witness asked him his reason for thinking that he had so many mortal enemies, and pannel replied, that they were goaded on by his wife—all his misfortunes were owing to that girl. Does not think that at the time of this conference he was under the influence of drink.

WM. MUIR has known the prisoner for 25 years or so. Met him in Hutchesontown in Nov. last ; saw him pull from his pocket a knife, and was asked if he had not seen these Irish b——s following him ? Witness told him he was labouring under a delusion. There was nobody following him. He insisted to the contrary, and said that his very brother had a design upon his life.

JOHN M'KAY, cotton-spinner, saw the pannel in M'Gown's house, the scene of the tragedy, on the day previous to its taking place. Asked him, when he came into the room where he was, How he did ? Pannel replied that he was pretty well, but it was a matter of no consequence whether he was so or not, for he had only 24 hours to live ; witness asked him how he arrived at that conclusion, and pannel answered, that there was a society existing, who possessed the power of life and death, and who had doomed him to die in the course of 24 hours at the farthest,—his time in this world might be shorter, but this, at all events, was its utmost extent. He did not appear to be the least the worse of liquor.

John M'Kean recollects a circumstance in the history of the pannel at the bar, which took place about six weeks before the melancholy death of his wife. About this time he went into a public house with the prisoner, when, after sitting a little time, he (pannel) ran out and brought into the room a person called Murdoch, on whom he poured forth the most violent abuse, charging him with having a criminal connection with his wife. Murdoch stated that he had never seen his wife to his knowledge, on which announcement he became in an instant perfectly calm.

Mr. Russel, counsel for the pannel, then informed the Court, that he had some other witnesses who could speak to similar facts, and to dates the same as those which had already been condescended on. He would, however, not detain the Jury longer, and would trust the fate of the unfortunate man at the bar on the evidence which had already been adduced in proof of his insanity. He would, however, examine one witness more, and that was Dr. Corkindale, who had already been heard in favour of the crown, and would call upon that learned gentleman now to state his opinion of the mind of his unhappy client, after having been present at the examination of all the witnesses.

Here Lord Meadowbank paid a high compliment to Mr. Russel, for the great talents which he had displayed on this occasion. He was speaking the sentiments of his learned brother as well as his own, when he said, that he had this day shown abilities which were not only highly honourable to himself, but conferred a lustre on the profession to which he belonged.

The Doctor, without being again sworn, but requested to consider himself still upon oath, then went into the box.

Mr. Russel.—Dr. Corkindale, after having heard the whole evidence which has been adduced upon this side of the bar, tending to prove the insanity of the prisoner at the time he committed the deed, do you, or do you not find reason to change the opinion which you formerly expressed?

Dr. Corkindale—I do not.

Mr. Russel—Do you mean to say that the evidence does not prove the unhappy man to have been at any time insane?

Dr. Corkindale—I observed no symptoms of insanity while the prisoner was under my charge in the Jail, but I think there is no reason to doubt, from the evidence, that he was insane in the months of March and April, 1825, and that this alienation of mind continued, with some variation, up to the time when the fatal deed was committed.

Mr. Russel—Was such alienation of a sort to render him irresponsible for his actions?

Dr. Corkindale—It occurs to me that the act of Campbell resembled very much that of Hatfield, who fired at the late King; which Lord Erskine defined to be " the immediate, unqualified offspring of a diseased delusion operating on the faculties with respect to one object, without obviously impairing the intellect on other topics at the same time." Jealousy of his wife latterly was in Campbell's case the delusion; which was no doubt enhanced by her own conduct; and I have no doubt, he plunged the knife into her bosom whilst labouring under a paroxysm of real insanity.

Lord Meadowbank—In the many cases, Doctor, which you have seen and attended, did you ever meet with such a sudden *cure*, as that which occurred in the case of the prisoner?

Dr. CORKINDALE—I have never met, my Lord, with such an extraordinary case as the present one; still, however, I do not doubt the possibility of such case. The object of the hallucination being accomplished, and punished n the death of his wife, and together with the long sleep which he enjoyd immediately afterwards, may have been sufficient to restore his faculties to oundness and tranquillity.

LORD M'KENZIE—Is the Court to understand then, from Dr. Corkindale, hat the prisoner did not know what he was doing; could not distinguish etween right and wrong, when he committed the deed?

Dr. CORKINDALE—He knew, my Lord, very well what he was doing; but e was compelled to the act by the ungovernable strength of a particular hallunation.

LORD M'KENZIE—It was more an insanity of the *will* than of the *intellect* nen?

Dr. CORKINDALE—No, my Lord. The intellect was eclipsed, upon a paricular subject, by a delusion, and the *will*, though perhaps sound in itself, as directed a wrong way by the insane intellect.

LORD MEADOWBANK—The act, then, was not the offspring of ungovernble passion excited in a *sound* mind; but of a passion, roused by circumstances, a *diseased* one?

Dr. CORKINDALE—Just so, my Lord. He had long been brooding on the eath either of himself or others; his particular hallucination was called ividly into action, by real circumstances, upon the night of the accident, and occurred, I have no doubt, in a fit of real frenzy.

The most intense interest was excited in the Court during this examination.

The DEPUTE-ADVOCATE then rose and said—Gentlemen of the Jury— t the conclusion of the evidence for the Crown in this case, no doubt reained in my mind that I would be called upon, in the discharge of my duty, claim for you a verdict of guilty against the unhappy man at the bar; but the termination of that which my learned friend has been enabled to pro- uce in behalf of the prisoner, I am happy to say that I can have as little oubt that you must return a very different verdict. At the commencement f the trial I had not the smallest conception that my learned friend on the pposite side of the bar could have made out such a case for the insanity of e prisoner when he committed the deed, as he has done, and that even together independent of the convincing testimony of my friend, Dr. Cork- dale, whose evidence, taken along with that of the preceding witnesses for e opposite side, I am free to confess, after the most assiduous and painful tention which I could give, leaves you but one duty to perform, and that is return a verdict, finding the prisoner guilty of the act charged in the in- ictment, but, at the same time, that when he committed it, he was labouring nder a *fit of insanity.*

Mr. RUSSEL—Gentlemen of the Jury.—After the speech of my learned iend, which you have just heard, nothing remains for me to do but to thank ou for that patient attention to the interesting details of this case which you ve exercised. I am exceedingly sorry for the time which has been spent in king the evidence, which I thought it my duty to bring forward in behalf of y client; but with my small experience in the business of this Court I shrunk from the responsibility of abridging it, and chose rather to encumber the case with too much, than run the awful hazard of injuring the interests of my client by bringing forward too little ; and may I not rest satisfied, that since the life of one fellow-creature had already been sacrificed, and that of another placed in jeopardy by the subject of your investigations, you will not grudge the trouble and time you have been called to employ? The candour of my learned friend in abandoning the case, after the evidence which you and he have just been attending to, meets my warmest thanks, though you can have now no doubt that in doing so, he did no more than his duty.—Gentlemen— Although my client escapes the punishment so justly due to the crime of murder, yet his lot is still an unhappy one. But, amidst all his unhappiness, he will still have the consolation of thinking that his misery is the misery of misfortune, not the writhing agony arising from the pangs of remorse.

Lord Meadowbank.—Gentlemen of the Jury—During the whole course of my experience in the business of this Court, I do not recollect of ever having met with a case which called for such a patient examination, or which kept the mind on such a painful stretch of excitement as the present one. So much was the subject beset with difficulties, that I must acknowledge, before the admirable evidence elicited from Dr. Corkindale, both my learned Brother and I were much at a loss what charge to give you, or what directions it was our duty to offer. But the valuable testimony of that very learned person has completely cleared away those difficulties, and made our path of duty both pleasant and open. You and I are both greatly indebted to him for his lucid and refreshing testimony, and if any thing can add to his reputation with his brethren and the public, it must be the proceedings of this day. The prisoner's counsel, too, must not pass without due praise for his admirable conduct in managing the case—his masterly measure of placing Dr. Corkindale again in that box, although he must have been perfectly sure of the candour, discretion, and gentlemanly feeling of that learned physician, deserves our highest commendation. The ability with which he has conducted the case does honour to himself and the profession to which he belongs. It could not have been excelled by the most experienced gentlemen at the bar; and wherever he acquired it, I am sure it was not from his duration or extent of practice in this Court. It would also be the greatest injustice to my friend, Mr. Dundas, not to mention, with praise, the able assistance which the Court has derived (as it always derives,) from his exertions in the progress of this case. His sole aim was to arrive at the truth, and in accomplishing it, he spared no pains and exercised the greatest patience. Gentlemen, you have heard what was suggested to you by the public prosecutor, and it remains now only for you to consider of your verdict. In the first place, you have to consider whether or not it was the prisoner who committed the deed libelled on. If any of you have the smallest doubt on that subject, it will be my duty to go over the evidence—[Here a general movement among the Jury indicated that they had no doubt]—but since you have not, it remains only for you to return your verdict. And as it is of importance that the verdict returned be such as can be received; and as the proper one may not at once occur to you, allow me to furnish you with a formula of what it ought to be.

Here his Lordship handed to the Jury the proper formula, which Lor

John Campbell, as Chancellor, read aloud as the verdict of the Jury :—Find the pannel Guilty of the crime charged, but that he was quite insane and deprived of his reason at the time he committed the deed.

The Court then sentenced him to be confined in Glasgow Jail all the days of his life ; at least aye and until his friends give security that he shall be prevented from hurting himself or any other person, and orders be given for his liberation by the Court.

Counsel for the Crown, ROBERT DUNDAS, ESQ.—for the Pannel, JOHN RUSSEL, ESQ.— Agent Mr. JOHN BURNET, Writer, Glasgow.